THE CELI

MAR

VERITAS PUBLICATIONS DUBLIN

MARRIAGE

In the Old Testament God often calls his people his "bride". Jesus, too, spoke of himself as the bridegroom. Paul speaks of the union of wife and husband in marriage as a profound mystery that "refers to Christ and the Church" (Eph 5:32). In the sacrament of matrimony the Christian man and woman exercise their priesthood together, conferring the sacrament on each other. Through their exchange of consent and the blessing of the Church, God seals their love. The relationship of sacramental marriage should show forth the love of God that binds him to mankind as husband and wife are united. The fidelity unto death of husband and wife reflects the eternal faithfulness of God to his promises. The family, which begins with marriage, is a sign of the great family of God.

ACKNOWLEDGEMENTS

The text of the Marriage Rite, as adapted by the Liturgical Commission of the Irish hierarchy in consultation with the International Committee on English in the Liturgy, and approved by the Irish Episcopal Conference and the Sacred Congregation for Divine Worship for official use in Ireland, is copyright © 1970, 1980 ✠Thomas Morris, the Catholic Communications Institute of Ireland, Inc.. All rights reserved.
The excerpts from the *Order of Mass*, with the exception of the Our Father, are copyright © 1969 and 1973, International Committee on English in the Liturgy, Inc.. All rights reserved.

Concordat cum originali: ✠Michael Harty, Bishop of Killaloe.

Imprimatur: ✠Dermot, Archbishop of Dublin, June 1980.

Reprinted 1984
Cover design by Steven Hope.
Typography by Liam Miller.
Symbols by Berthold Wolpe.

ISBN 0 86217 011 7
Cat. No. 3520

Printed in the Republic of Ireland
by Paceprint Ltd.

INTRODUCTORY RITES

The priest may greet and welcome the bride and bridegroom at the door of the church or at the altar. The entrance antiphon may be sung or recited, or a hymn may be sung.

ENTRANCE ANTIPHON   Ps 19:3, 5

1] May the Lord send you help from his holy place and from Zion may he watch over you. May he grant you your heart's desire and lend his aid to all your plans.

or   Ps 89:14, 17

2] Fill us with your love, O Lord, and we will sing for joy all our days. May the goodness of the Lord be upon us, and give success to the work of our hands.

or   Ps 144:2, 9

3] Lord, I will bless you day after day, and praise your name for ever; for you are kind to all, and compassionate to all your creatures.

THE GREETING

P In the name of the Father, and of the Son, and of the Holy Spirit.

C **Amen.**

Then the priest greets the people.

1] P The grace of our Lord Jesus Christ and the love of God and the fellowship of the Holy Spirit be with you all.

C **And also with you.**

or

2] P The grace and peace of God our Father and the Lord Jesus Christ be with you.

C **Blessed be God, the Father of our Lord Jesus Christ.**

or

C **And also with you.**

or

3] P The Lord be with you.

C **And also with you.**

1

PENITENTIAL RITE

The priest invites the people to ask God to forgive their sins in these or similar words:

P   My brothers and sisters,
      to prepare ourselves to celebrate the sacred mysteries,
      let us call to mind our sins.

After a brief silence, all make the same prayer for forgiveness, using one of the following forms.

1] *first form*

P C **I confess to almighty God,**
      and to you, my brothers and sisters,
      that I have sinned through my own fault

they strike their breast

      in my thoughts and in my words,
      in what I have done,
      and in what I have failed to do;
      and I ask blessed Mary, ever virgin,
      all the angels and saints,
      and you, my brothers and sisters,
      to pray for me to the Lord our God.

2] *or second form*

P   Lord, we have sinned against you:
      Lord, have mercy.

C   **Lord, have mercy.**

P   Lord, show us your mercy and love.

C   **And grant us your salvation.**

3] *or third form*

P   You were sent to heal the contrite:
      Lord, have mercy.

C   **Lord, have mercy.**

P   You came to call sinners:
      Christ, have mercy.

C   **Christ, have mercy.**

P   You plead for us at the right hand of the Father:
      Lord, have mercy.

C   **Lord, have mercy.**

Then the priest says the absolution.

P   May almighty God have mercy on us,
     forgive us our sins,
     and bring us to everlasting life.

C **Amen.**

The invocations, Lord, have mercy, *follow unless they have already been used in one of the forms of the act of penance.*

P Lord, have mercy.	C **Lord, have mercy.**
P Christ, have mercy.	C **Christ, have mercy.**
P Lord, have mercy.	C **Lord, have mercy.**

THE GLORIA

P Glory to God in the highest,

PC **and peace to his people on earth.**
    Lord God, heavenly King,
    almighty God and Father,
      we worship you, we give you thanks,
      we praise you for your glory.

    Lord Jesus Christ, only Son of the Father,
    Lord God, Lamb of God,
    you take away the sin of the world:
      have mercy on us;
    you are seated at the right hand of the Father:
      receive our prayer.
    For you alone are the Holy One,
    you alone are the Lord,
    you alone are the Most High,
      Jesus Christ,
      with the Holy Spirit,
      in the glory of God the Father.   Amen.

P   Let us pray.
Priest and people pray silently for a while.
Then the priest says the opening prayer.
Any of the following forms may be used.

1]   *first form*
P   Father,
    you have made the bond of marriage
    a holy mystery,
    a symbol of Christ's love for his Church.
    Hear our prayers for N. and N.
    With faith in you and in each other
    they pledge their love today.
    May their lives always bear witness
    to the reality of that love.
    We ask this through our Lord Jesus Christ, your Son,
    who lives and reigns with you and the Holy Spirit,
    one God, for ever and ever.
C   **Amen.**

Turn to page 5.

2]   *or second form*
P   Father,
    when you created mankind
    you willed that man and wife should be one.
    Bind N. and N.
    in the loving union of marriage
    and make their love fruitful
    so that they may be living witnesses
    to your divine love in the world.
    We ask this through our Lord Jesus Christ, your Son,
    who lives and reigns with you and the Holy Spirit,
    one God, for ever and ever.
C   **Amen.**

Turn to page 5.

3] *or third form*

P   Father,
> hear our prayers for N. and N.,
> who today are united in marriage before your altar.
> Give them your blessing,
> and strengthen their love for each other.

> We ask this through our Lord Jesus Christ, your Son
> who lives and reigns with you and the Holy Spirit,
> one God, for ever and ever.

C   **Amen.**

4] *or fourth form*

P   Almighty God,
> hear our prayers for N. and N.,
> who have come here today
> to be united in the sacrament of marriage.
> Increase their faith in you and in each other,
> and through them bless your Church (with Christian
>   children).

> We ask this through our Lord Jesus Christ, your Son,
> who lives and reigns with you and the Holy Spirit,
> one God, for ever and ever.

C   **Amen.**

LITURGY OF THE WORD

There may be three readings in the Liturgy of the Word, the first of them from the Old Testament. It is recommended that the bride and bridegroom choose the readings to be used.

The Gospel is always followed by a homily. This will treat of such themes as the mystery of Christian marriage, the dignity of married love, the grace of the sacrament and the responsibilities of married people.

THE RITE OF MARRIAGE

All stand, including the bride and bridegroom, whom the priest now addresses. He may use either of the three forms given below or he may make his own adaptation of them.

ADDRESS

1] *first form*

P   Dear children of God, you have come to this church so that the Lord may seal your love in the presence of the priest and this community.

Christian marriage is a sacred union which enriches natural love. It binds those who enter it to be faithful to each other for ever; it creates between them a bond that endures for life and cannot be broken; it demands that they love and honour each other, (that they accept from God the children he may give them, and bring them up in his love).
To help them in their marriage the husband and wife receive the life-long grace of the sacrament.

Is this your understanding of marriage?

Both   It is.

2] *or second form*

P   Dear children of God, you have come to this church so that the Lord may seal your love in the presence of the priest and this community. Christ blesses this love. He has already consecrated you in baptism; now, by a special sacrament, he strengthens you to fulfil the duties of your married life.

6

The priest then questions the bride and bridegroom.

P   N. and N. you are about to celebrate this sacrament.
Have you come here of your own free will and choice
and without compulsion to marry each other ?

Both   We have.

P   Will you love and honour each other in marriage all
the days of your life ?

Both   We will.

*The following question may be omitted if, for example, the
couple is advanced in years.*

P   Are you willing to accept with love the children God
may send you and bring them up in accordance with
the law of Christ and his Church ?

Both   We are.

3]   *or third form*

P   Dear children of God,

You have come today to pledge your love before God
and before the Church here present in the person of the
priest, your families and friends.

In becoming husband and wife you give yourselves to
each other for life. You promise to be true and faithful,
to support and cherish each other until death, so that
your years together will be the living out in love of the
pledge you now make. May your love for each other
reflect the enduring love of Christ for his Church.
As you face the future together, keep in mind that the
Sacrament of marriage unites you with Christ, and
brings you, through the years, the grace and blessing
of God our Father. Marriage is from God: he alone
can give you the happiness which goes beyond human
expectation, and which grows deeper through the
difficulties and struggles of life.

Put your trust in God as you set out together in life.
Make your home a centre of Christian family life. (In
this you will bequeath to your children a heritage
more lasting than temporal wealth).

The Christian home makes Christ and his Church present in the world of everyday things. May all who enter your home find there the presence of the Lord; for he has said: "Where two or three are gathered together in my name, there am I in the midst of them."

P Now, as you are about to exchange your marriage vows the Church wishes to be assured that you appreciate the meaning of what you do, and so I ask you: Have you come here of your own free will and choice to marry each other ?

Both We have.

P Will you love and honour each other in marriage all the days of your life ?

Both We will.

P Are you willing to accept with love the children God may send you, and bring them up in accordance with the law of Christ, and his Church ?

Both We are.

DECLARATION OF CONSENT
The priest then invites the couple to declare their consent.
He may use any of the four forms given below.

1] *first form*

P I invite you then to declare before God and his Church your consent to become husband and wife.

Bridegroom N., do you consent to be my wife ?
Bride I do. Do you, N., consent to be my husband ?
Bridegroom I do.
Bridegroom I take you as my wife
and I give myself to you as your husband
Bride I take you as my husband
and I give myself to you as your wife

They then join hands and say together:
to love each other truly
for better, for worse,
for richer, for poorer,
in sickness and in health,
till death do us part. (*or* all the days of our life.)

8

When the bride and bridegroom have given their consent the priest says:

P   What God joins together
    man must not separate.

May the Lord confirm the consent that you have given
and enrich you with his blessings.

Turn to page 12.

2]   *or second form*

P   I invite you then to declare before God and his Church
    your consent to become husband and wife.

They join hands.

Bridegroom   I, N., take you, N., as my wife,
              for better, for worse,
              for richer, for poorer,
              in sickness and in health,
              till death do us part.
              (*or* all the days of our life.)

Bride   I, N., take you, N., as my husband
         for better, for worse,
         for richer, for poorer,
         in sickness and in health,
         till death do us part.
         (*or* all the days of our life.)

When the bride and bridegroom have given their consent the priest says:

          P   What God joins together
              man must not separate.
              May the Lord confirm the consent that you
              have given
              and enrich you with his blessings.

Turn to page 12.

3]   *or third form*

P   I invite you then to declare before God and his Church
    your consent to become husband and wife.

They join hands. The priest then asks the bridegroom:

P N., do you take N. as your wife,
 for better, for worse,
 for richer, for poorer,
 in sickness and in health,
 till death do you part ?
 (*or* all the days of your life ?)

Bridegroom I do.

The priest then asks the bride:

P N., do you take N. as your husband,
 for better, for worse,
 for richer, for poorer,
 in sickness and in health,
 till death do you part ?
 (*or* all the days of your life ?)

Bride I do.
P What God joins together
 man must not separate.

May the Lord confirm the consent that you
 have given
and enrich you with his blessings.

Turn to page 12.

4] *or fourth form*

P I invite you then to declare before God and his
 Church your decision to become husband
 and wife.

Bridegroom N., Do you consent to be my wife ?
Bride I do.
Bride N., Do you consent to be my husband ?
Bridegroom I do.

They join hands and say together:

We take each other as husband and wife
and promise to love each other truly

for better, for worse,
for richer, for poorer,
in sickness and health,
till death do us part.
(*or* all the days of our life.)

P   The Lord has joined you together. May he
fulfil his blessing in you; may he keep you
in his love.

BLESSING OF RINGS
*The priest then blesses the ring or rings using any of the four
forms given below.*

1] *first form*
P   Lord, bless ✠ N. and N. and consecrate their
married life.
May this ring (these rings) be a symbol of their
faith in each other, and a reminder of their
love.
Through Christ our Lord.
Both   Amen.

2] *or second form*
P   May the Lord bless ✠ this ring (these rings)
which will be the sign of your love and
fidelity.
Both   Amen.

3] *or third form*
P   Lord, bless ✠ these rings.
Grant that those who wear them
may always be faithful to each other.
May they do your will
and live in peace with you in mutual love.
Through Christ our Lord.
Both   Amen.

4] *or fourth form*

P   Almighty God, bless this ring (these rings),
           ⊬ symbol(s) of faithfulness and unbroken
              love.
        May N. and N. always be true to each other,
        may they be one in heart and mind,
        may they be united in love forever,
        Through Christ, our Lord.

Both   Amen.

The bridegroom places the bride's ring on her finger.
He may say:
N., wear this ring as a sign of our faithful love.*
In the name of the Father, and of the Son, and of the Holy
Spirit.

The bride may place a ring on the bridegroom's finger.
She may say:
N., wear this ring as a sign of our faithful love.*
In the name of the Father, and of the Son, and of the Holy
Spirit.

The bridegroom may give gold and silver to the bride, saying:
        I give you this gold and silver,
        tokens of all I possess.

or
The bride and groom may exchange small symbolic gifts
saying:
        N., I give you this gift,
        a token of all I possess.

or *N., wear this ring as a sign of our love and fidelity.

PRAYER OF THE NEWLY MARRIED COUPLE*

The couple are recommended to say together the following or some similar prayer:

We thank you, Lord,
and we praise you
for bringing us
to this happy day.

You have given us to each other.
Now, together, we give ourselves to you.
We ask you, Lord:
make us one in our love;
keep us one in your peace.

Protect our marriage.
Bless our home.
Make us gentle.
Keep us faithful.

And when life is over
unite us again
where parting is no more
in the kingdom of your love.

There we will praise you
in the happiness and peace
of our eternal home.
Amen.

PRAYER OF THE FAITHFUL

The prayer of the faithful follows. Some of the following intercessions may be used or others devised.

Reader 1 For N. and N. that the Lord,
who has brought them to this happy day
will keep them forever
in fidelity and love,
let us pray to the Lord. (*Repeat after each intercession*).

C Lord, hear our prayer. (*Repeat after each intercession*)

* Alternatively, the prayer may be said before or after the prayer after communion.

2 For the parents of N. and N., for their friends
and all who have helped them
to become husband and wife,

3 That the Lord may bless the world with his peace
and the protection of his love,

4 For our community and our families,
who welcome Christ into their lives;
that they learn to receive him
in the poor and suffering people of this world,

5 For God's Church, the Bride of Christ,
that it may be united in faith and love,

6 For all who are victims of injustice,
and for those deprived of love and affection,

7 For married couples everywhere
that their lives will be an example to the world
of unity, fidelity and love,

8 For those who mourn, while we are rejoicing,
that in their suffering and loneliness
they may experience the strength of God's
support,

9 For the faithful departed
and especially for those
whom we, ourselves, have loved,
that God will one day unite us again
in the joys of our eternal home,

PROFESSION OF FAITH

*The Creed, if it is to be recited, follows the prayer of the
faithful.*

LITURGY OF THE EUCHARIST

*The bride and bridegroom may bring the bread and wine to the
altar. The preparation of the gifts continues in the usual way.*

The priest invites the people to pray.

P   Pray, brethren, that our sacrifice
     may be acceptable to God, the almighty Father.

C   **May the Lord accept the sacrifice at your hands**
     for the praise and glory of his name,
     for our good, and the good of all his Church.

The priest then says the prayer over the gifts.
Any of the following three forms may be used.

1] *first form*

P   Lord,
     accept our offering
     for this newly married couple, N. and N.
     By your love and providence you have brought them
        together;
     now bless them all the days of their married life.
     We ask this through Christ our Lord.   C **Amen.**

2] *or second form*

P   Lord,
     accept the gifts we offer you
     on this happy day.
     In your fatherly love
     watch over and protect N. and N.,
     whom you have united in marriage.
     We ask this through Christ our Lord.   C **Amen.**

3] *or third form*

P   Lord,
     hear our prayers
     and accept the gifts we offer for N. and N.
     Today you have made them one in the sacrament of
        marriage.
     May the mystery of Christ's unselfish love,
     which we celebrate in this eucharist,
     increase their love for you and for each other.
     We ask this through Christ our Lord.   C **Amen.**

THE EUCHARISTIC PRAYER

Any of the four eucharistic prayers may be used. Eucharistic Prayer I is given below as it contains special forms.

P   The Lord be with you.
C   **And also with you.**
P   Lift up your hearts.
C   **We lift them up to the Lord.**
P   Let us give thanks to the Lord our God.
C   **It is right to give him thanks and praise.**

There are three special prefaces for marriage and normally one of these will be used.

PREFACE

1] *first form*
P   Father, all-powerful and ever-living God,
     we do well always and everywhere to give you thanks.

     By this sacrament your grace unites man and woman
     in an unbreakable bond of love and peace.

     You have designed the chaste love of husband and wife
     for the increase both of the human family
     and of your own family born in baptism.

     You are the loving Father of the world of nature;
     You are the loving Father of the new creation of grace.
     In Christian marriage you bring together the two orders
        of creation;
     nature's gift of children enriches the world
     and your grace enriches also your Church.
     Through Christ the choirs of angels
     and all the saints
     praise and worship your glory.
     May our voices blend with theirs
     as we join in their unending hymn:

Turn to page 18.

2] *or second form*

P   Father, all-powerful and ever-living God,
    we do well always and everywhere to give you thanks
    through Jesus Christ our Lord.

Through him you entered into a new covenant with
    your people.

You restored man to grace in the saving mystery of
    redemption.

You gave him a share in the divine life
through his union with Christ.

You made him an heir of Christ's eternal glory.

This outpouring of love in the new covenant of grace
is symbolised in the marriage covenant
that seals the love of husband and wife
and reflects your divine plan of love.

And so, with the angels and all the saints in heaven,
we proclaim your glory
    and join in their unending hymn of praise:

Turn to page 18.

3] *or third form*

P   Father, all-powerful and ever-living God,
    we do well always and everywhere to give you thanks.

You created man in love to share your divine life.
We see his high destiny in the love of husband and
wife, which bears the imprint of your own divine love.

Love is man's origin,
love is his constant calling,
love is his fulfilment in heaven.

The love of man and woman
is made holy in the sacrament of marriage,
and becomes the mirror of your everlasting love.

Through Christ the choirs of angels
and all the saints
praise and worship your glory.

May our voices blend with theirs
as we join in their unending hymn:

PC **Holy, holy, holy Lord, God of power and might,**
heaven and earth are full of your glory.
Hosanna in the highest.
Blessed is he who comes in the name of the Lord.
Hosanna in the highest.

P We come to you, Father,
with praise and thanksgiving,
through Jesus Christ your Son.
Through him we ask you to accept and bless ✠
these gifts we offer you in sacrifice.

We offer them for your holy catholic Church,
watch over it, Lord, and guide it;
grant it peace and unity throughout the world.
We offer them for N. our Pope,
for N. our bishop,
and for all who hold and teach the catholic faith
that comes to us from the apostles.

Remember, Lord, your people,
especially those for whom we now pray, N. and N..
Remember all of us gathered here before you.
You know how firmly we believe in you
and dedicate ourselves to you.
We offer you this sacrifice of praise
for ourselves and those who are dear to us.
We pray to you, our living and true God,
for our well-being and redemption.

In union with the whole Church
we honour Mary,
the ever-virgin mother of Jesus Christ our Lord and
    God.
We honour Joseph, her husband,
the apostles and martyrs
Peter and Paul, Andrew,

18

(James, John, Thomas,
James, Philip,
Bartholomew, Matthew, Simon and Jude;
we honour Linus, Cletus, Clement, Sixtus,
Cornelius, Cyprian, Lawrence, Chrysogonus,
John and Paul, Cosmas and Damian)
and all the saints.
May their merits and prayers
gain us your constant help and protection.
(Through Christ our Lord.   Amen.)

Father, accept this offering
from your whole family
and from N. and N. for whom we now pray.
You have brought them to their wedding day:
grant them (the gift and joy of children and)
a long and happy life together.
(Through Christ our Lord.   Amen.)

Bless and approve our offering;
make it acceptable to you,
an offering in spirit and in truth.
Let it become for us
the body and blood of Jesus Christ,
your only Son, our Lord.

The day before he suffered
he took bread in his sacred hands
and looking up to heaven,
to you, his almighty Father,
he gave you thanks and praise.
He broke the bread,
gave it to his disciples, and said:
TAKE THIS, ALL OF YOU, AND EAT IT:
THIS IS MY BODY WHICH WILL BE GIVEN UP FOR
    YOU.

When supper was ended
he took the cup.
Again he gave you thanks and praise,
gave the cup to his disciples, and said:
TAKE THIS, ALL OF YOU, AND DRINK FROM IT:
THIS IS THE CUP OF MY BLOOD,
THE BLOOD OF THE NEW AND EVERLASTING
COVENANT.
IT WILL BE SHED FOR YOU AND FOR ALL MEN
SO THAT SINS MAY BE FORGIVEN.
DO THIS IN MEMORY OF ME.

ACCLAMATION OF THE PEOPLE
P   Let us proclaim the mystery of faith.
C   **Christ has died,**
    Christ is risen,
    Christ will come again. (*or alternative forms*)

P   Father, we celebrate the memory of Christ your Son.
    We, your people and your ministers,
    recall his passion,
    his resurrection from the dead,
    and his ascension into glory;
    and from the many gifts you have given us
    we offer to you, God of glory and majesty,
    this holy and perfect sacrifice:
    the bread of life
    and the cup of eternal salvation.

    Look with favour on these offerings
    and accept them as once you accepted
    the gifts of your servant Abel,
    the sacrifice of Abraham, our father in faith,
    and the bread and wine offered by your priest
       Melchisedech.

Almighty God,
we pray that your angel may take this sacrifice
to your altar in heaven.
Then, as we receive from this altar
the sacred body and blood of your Son,
let us be filled with every grace and blessing.
(Through Christ our Lord. Amen.)

Remember, Lord, those who have died
and have gone before us marked with the sign of faith,
especially those for whom we now pray, N. and N..
May these, and all who sleep in Christ,
find in your presence
light, happiness, and peace.
(Through Christ our Lord. Amen.)

For ourselves, too, we ask
some share in the fellowship of your apostles and
    martyrs,
with John the Baptist, Stephen, Matthias, Barnabas,
(Ignatius, Alexander, Marcellinus, Peter,
Felicity, Perpetua, Agatha, Lucy,
Agnes, Cecilia, Anastasia)
and all the saints.
Though we are sinners,
we trust in your mercy and love.
Do not consider what we truly deserve,
but grant us your forgiveness.
Through Christ our Lord
you give us all these gifts.
You fill them with life and goodness,
you bless them and make them holy.

Through him, with him, in him,
in the unity of the Holy Spirit,
all glory and honour is yours, almighty Father,
for ever and ever.

C **Amen.**

COMMUNION RITE

THE LORD'S PRAYER

The priest invites the people to pray in these or similar words:

P   Let us pray with confidence to the Father
in the words our Saviour gave us:

PC **Our Father, who art in heaven,
hallowed be thy name.
Thy kingdom come.
Thy will be done on earth, as it is in heaven.
Give us this day our daily bread,
and forgive us our trespasses,
as we forgive those who trespass against us,
and lead us not into temptation,
but deliver us from evil.**

NUPTIAL BLESSING

*Immediately after the Lord's Prayer, the priest faces the bride
and bridegroom and blesses them, using one of the following
four forms. Words in brackets may be omitted.*

1] *first form*

P   Let us ask God to bless N. and N., now married in
Christ,
and unite them in his love
(through the sacrament of his body and blood).

Silent prayer. Then the priest continues:

God, our Father, creator of the universe,
you made man and woman in your own likeness,
and blessed their union.
We humbly pray to you for this bridegroom and bride,
today united in the sacrament of marriage.

22

May your blessing come upon them.
May they find happiness in their love for each other,
(be blessed in their children,)
and enrich the life of the Church.
May they praise you in their days of happiness
and turn to you in times of sorrow.
May they know the joy of your help in their work
and the strength of your presence in their need.
May they worship you with the Church
and be your witnesses in the world.
May old age come to them in the company of their
    friends,
and may they reach at last the kingdom of heaven.
We ask this through Christ our Lord.

C   **Amen.**
Turn to p. 26.

2]   *or second form*
P   Let us ask God to bless N. and N. now married in Christ
and unite them in his love
(through the sacrament of his body and blood.)
Silent prayer.   *Then the priest continues:*
Father, you created the universe
and made man and woman in your own likeness.
You gave woman as companion to man
so that they should no longer be two, but one flesh,
teaching us that those you have so united may never be
    separated.
Father, you have sanctified marriage in a mystery so holy
that it is a sign of the union of Christ and his Church.
Look with love upon N., as she asks your blessing.
May she live in peace with you
and follow the example of those women
whose lives are praised in the scriptures.
May N. place his trust in her
and see her as his companion.

May he always honour her
and love her as Christ loves the Church.
Father, keep this husband and wife strong in faith
and true to your commandments.
May they be faithful to each other,
examples of Christian living,
and witnesses of Christ.
(Bless them with children and help them to be good
    parents.)
And, after a long and happy life together,
may they enjoy the company of your saints in heaven.
We ask this through Christ our Lord.

C   **Amen.** *Turn to p.* 26.

3]   *or third form*

P   Let us pray to the Lord for N. and N.,
who as they begin their married life
come to God's altar to deepen their love
(by sharing in the body and blood of Christ.)

Silent prayer. Then the priest continues:

Father, you created man and woman in your own image
and united them in body and heart
so that they might fulfil your plan for the world.
To reveal your loving design,
you made the union of man and wife
a sign of the covenant between you and your people;
through the sacrament of marriage you perfect this
    union
and make it now a sign of Christ's love for his bride the
    Church.
Lord, bless this husband and wife and protect them.
Grant that as they live this sacrament
they may learn to share with each other the gifts of your
    love.
May they become one in heart and mind
as witnesses to your presence in their marriage.
(Bless them with children

who will be formed by the gospel and have a place in
   your family in heaven.)
May N. be a good wife (and mother),
caring for her home,
faithful to her husband,
generous and kind.
May N. be a good husband (and a devoted father),
gentle and strong,
faithful to his wife,
and a careful provider for his household.
Father, grant that, as they now come as man and wife to
your altar,
they may one day share your feast in heaven.
We ask this through Christ our Lord.

C **Amen.**   *Turn to p.* 26.

4]   *or fourth form*
P   We call God our Father. Let each of us now ask him,
   in silence, to bless these his children as they begin their
   married life.
Silent prayer. Then the priest continues:
   Father,
   from you every family in heaven and earth takes its
      name.
   You made us.
   You made all that exists.
   You made man and woman like yourself in their power
      to know and love.
   You call them to share life with each other, saying "It is
      not good for man to be alone".
   (You bless them with children to give new life to
      your people, telling them: "Increase and multiply,
      and fill the earth.")
   We call to mind the fruitful companionship of
      Abraham, our father in faith and his wife Sarah.
   We remember how your guiding hand brought
      Rebecca and Isaac together, and how through the

lives of Jacob and Rachel you prepared the way for the kingdom.

Father, you take delight in the love of husband and wife, that love which hopes and shares, heals and forgives. We ask you to bless N. and N. as they set out on their new life.

Fill their hearts with your holy Spirit, the Spirit of understanding, joy, fortitude and peace.

Strengthen them to do your will, and in the trials of life to bear the cross with Christ.

May they praise you during the bright days, and call on you in times of trouble.

(May their children bring them your blessing, and give glory to your name).

Let their love be strong as death,
a fire that floods cannot drown,
a jewel beyond all price.

May their life together give witness to their faith in Christ.

May they see long and happy days,
and be united forever in the kingdom of your glory.
We ask this through Christ our Lord.

C **Amen.**

The priest continues:

P Lord Jesus Christ, you said to your apostles:
I leave you peace, my peace I give you.
Look not on our sins, but on the faith of your Church,
and grant us the peace and unity of your kingdom
where you live for ever and ever.

C **Amen.**

P The peace of the Lord be with you always.
C **And also with you**.

The priest may then say:

P Let us offer each other the sign of peace.

According to local custom, the bride and bridegroom, and all present, offer each other a sign of peace and unity.

26

The priest then takes the host, breaks it over the paten and puts a small fragment in the chalice. As he does so the people say:

C **Lamb of God, you take away the sins of the world: have mercy on us.**

   Lamb of God, you take away the sins of the world: have mercy on us.

   Lamb of God, you take away the sins of the world: grant us peace.

The priest then invites the people to communion.

P This is the Lamb of God
   who takes away the sins of the world.
   Happy are those who are called to his supper.

PC **Lord, I am not worthy to receive you,
    but only say the word and I shall be healed.**

The communion now follows. The bride and bridegroom may receive communion under both kinds.

During communion it is recommended that a hymn be sung. If no hymn is sung the communion antiphon should be recited either by the people or by a reader or by the priest himself.

COMMUNION ANTIPHON   Eph 5:25-27
1] Christ loves his Church, and he sacrificed himself for
   her so that she could become like a holy and untouched
   bride.

---

or   Jn 13:34
2] I give you a new commandment: love one another as I
   have loved you, says the Lord.

---

or   Ps 33:1, 9
3] I will bless the Lord at all times, his praise shall be
   ever on my lips. Taste and see the goodness of the
   Lord; blessed is he who hopes in God.

If the prayer on page 13 has not been said, it may be said at this point.

PRAYER AFTER COMMUNION
P Let us pray.
Priest and people pray silently for a while.
Then the priest says the prayer after communion.
Any of the following forms may be used.

1] *first form*
P   Lord,
    in your love
    you have given us this eucharist
    to unite us with one another and with you.
    As you have made N. and N.
    one in this sacrament of marriage
    (and in the sharing of the one bread and the one cup),
    so now make them one in love for each other.
    We ask this through Christ our Lord.
C   **Amen.**

2] *or second form*
P   Lord,
    we who have shared the food of your table
    pray for our friends N. and N.,
    whom you have joined together in marriage.
    Keep them close to you always.
    May their love for each other
    proclaim to all the world
    their faith in you.
    We ask this through Christ our Lord.
C   **Amen.**

3] *or third form*
P   Almighty God,
    may the sacrifice we have offered
    and the eucharist we have shared
    strengthen the love of N. and N.,
    and give us all your fatherly aid.
    We ask this through Christ our Lord.
C   **Amen.**

The register may now be signed at some suitable place in or near the sanctuary.

CONCLUDING RITE

P   The Lord be with you.
C   **And also with you.**
Before blessing the people at the end of Mass, the priest gives the bride and bridegroom a special blessing. Any of the following forms may be used.

1] *first form*
P   May God, the eternal Father, keep you steadfast in
    your love.
C   **Amen.**
P   May you have children to bless you,
    friends to console you,
    and may you live in peace with all men.
C   **Amen.**
P   May you bear witness among men to the love of God.
    May the suffering and the poor find you generous
    and welcome you one day into our Father's kingdom.
C   **Amen.**
P   May the peace of Christ ever dwell in your home.
    May the angels of God protect it,
    and may the holy family of Nazareth be its model
    and inspiration.
C   **Amen.**

2] *or second form*
P   May God, the almighty Father, grant you his joy:
    may he bless you in your children.
C   **Amen.**
P   May Jesus Christ, the Son of God, in his mercy
    help you in good times and in bad.
C   **Amen.**
P   May the Holy Spirit of God
    always fill you with his love.
C   **Amen.**

29

3] *or third form*

P The Lord Jesus was present at the wedding in Cana;
today may he bless you and your families and friends.

C **Amen.**

P He loved his Church to the end;
may he fill your hearts to overflowing with his love.

C **Amen.**

P May he give you the grace to bear witness to his
resurrection,
and look forward to his coming with hope and joy.

C **Amen.**

P May the peace of Christ ever dwell in your home;
may the angels of God protect it,
and may the holy family of Nazareth be its model
and inspiration.

C **Amen.**

BLESSING AND DISMISSAL

P May almighty God bless you,
the Father, and the Son, ✠ and the Holy Spirit.

C **Amen.**

P The Mass is ended, go in peace.
or
Go in the peace of Christ.
or
Go in peace to love and serve the Lord.

C **Thanks be to God.**